NO KIDDING, MERMAIDS ARE A JOKE!

The Story of **THE LITTLE MERMAID**

as Told by **THE PRINCE**

by Nancy Loewen

illustrated by Amit Tayal

PICTURE WINDOW BOOKS
a capstone imprint

Special thanks to our adviser, Terry Flaherty, PhD, Professor of English,
Minnesota State University, Mankato, for his expertise.

Editor: Jill Kalz
Designer: Lori Bye
Art Director: Nathan Gassman
Production Specialist: Kathy McColley
The illustrations in this book were created digitally.

Picture Window Books
1710 Roe Crest Drive
North Mankato, MN 56003
www.capstonepub.com

Library of Congress Cataloging-in-Publication Data
Cataloging-in-publication information is on file with the Library of Congress.
ISBN 978-1-4048-8303-1 (library binding)
ISBN 978-1-4795-1947-7 (paper over board)
ISBN 978-1-4795-1951-4 (paperback)
ISBN 978-1-4795-1894-4 (eBook PDF)

Printed in the United States of America
in Stevens Point, Wisconsin.
032012   007227WZF13

Are mermaids *real?*

A little while ago, I would have said NO WAY! Sea creatures with people faces and people arms but great big fish tails instead of legs? That's nuts!

Then I met this girl ...

My name is Prince Aleck. I'll admit, I'm sort of a practical joker. If you're looking for someone to put chili powder in the toothpaste, or to glue coins to sidewalks, I'm your guy.

But back to the girl ... I found her on the shore one morning, just lying there. She was wiggling her toes as if she'd never seen them before.

She couldn't talk, but she drew pictures in the sand.
They were pretty wild.

She drew a merman king on a throne ...

and a mean-looking sea witch ...

and a mermaid drinking a potion ...

and then she drew that same
mermaid girl, with human legs.

7

I was a little suspicious. Here's why:

Not long ago, I had a birthday party on my dad's ship. That night a terrible storm came up, and the ship broke apart. Everyone else got on a lifeboat, but the wind tossed me into the water. I had this weird dream that someone carried me through the water—someone with long, flowing hair ... and a tail.

Or was it a dream? I woke up the next morning on a distant beach. I didn't know how I'd gotten there.

Anyway, I made the mistake of telling my buddies. They've been teasing me ever since. I can't go for a swim without someone tossing a doll in the water. I have to check my oatmeal for fish scales.

"Did Dave put you up to this?" I asked the girl. "Or Jimmy? I bet it was Jimmy."

She looked confused.

9

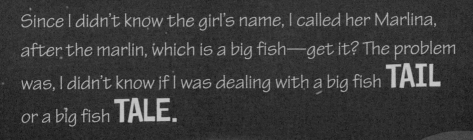

Since I didn't know the girl's name, I called her Marlina, after the marlin, which is a big fish—get it? The problem was, I didn't know if I was dealing with a big fish **TAIL** or a big fish **TALE.**

I sure liked her, though. Everyone liked Marlina. She was great at charades. She could teach kids to swim and dive in no time.

And she blew us away at the local dance contest.

Still, I couldn't shake the feeling that my buddies were playing a trick on me. Especially when they said things like, "Your girlfriend's quite a catch" or "Aleck and Marlina, swimming in the sea,

K-I-S-S-I-N-G."

So I came up with a test.

Remember my birthday party? When I washed up on that beach? A girl from a nearby school had helped me out. She'd let me use her cell phone to call home. Her name was Kim. I texted her.

KIM

Want 2 B on TV?
B famous?
Got a deal for U.

13

I took Kim along to royal events. I drew hearts around her name in the sand. I wrote letters to her on fancy paper and sealed them with a kiss.

I sighed a lot and got really good at making goo-goo eyes.

I still hung out with Marlina. But I made it clear
we were just friends. "What a pal," I told her.

My parents were thrilled. "See, honey?" my mom said to my dad. "I told you he'd grow up sooner or later!"

This is what I expected to happen:

As soon as I was married, my friends, and Marlina, would admit that the mermaid thing was a joke. Then I would admit that I wasn't really married. The wedding was a fake! We'd have a good laugh, and life would go on as usual—or it would, once my parents got over being mad.

This is what *actually* happened:

I got fake-married. My friends gave me a nose-shaped pencil sharpener and a case of chattering teeth as wedding gifts.

Marlina disappeared.

After the fake-wedding dance, for a split second, I thought I saw Marlina's face bobbing in the sea, far away. But when I blinked and looked again, all I saw was a bit of sea foam.

So, you tell me: Are mermaids real?

Don't tell anyone I said this, but my hunch is that they are.

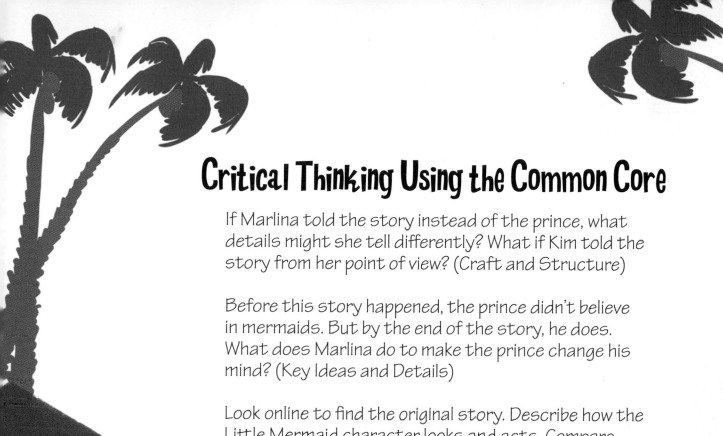

Critical Thinking Using the Common Core

If Marlina told the story instead of the prince, what details might she tell differently? What if Kim told the story from her point of view? (Craft and Structure)

Before this story happened, the prince didn't believe in mermaids. But by the end of the story, he does. What does Marlina do to make the prince change his mind? (Key Ideas and Details)

Look online to find the original story. Describe how the Little Mermaid character looks and acts. Compare and contrast her with Marlina in this version of the story. (Integration of Knowledge and Ideas)

Glossary

character—a person, animal, or creature in a story
point of view—a way of looking at something
version—an account of something from a certain point of view

Read More

Larkin, Rochelle, edited by. *The Little Mermaid & Other Stories*. Great Illustrated Classics. Edina, Minn.: Abdo Pub., 2005.

McFadden, Deanna. *The Little Mermaid*. Silver Penny Stories. New York: Sterling Children's Books, 2013.

Saxton, Patricia. *The Book of Mermaids*. Summit, N.J.: Shenanigan Books, 2006.

Internet Sites

FactHound offers a safe, fun way to find Internet sites related to this book. All of the sites on FactHound have been researched by our staff.

Here's all you do:
Visit *www.facthound.com*
Type in this code: 9781404883031

Look for all the books in the series:

Believe Me, Goldilocks Rocks!
Frankly, I Never Wanted to Kiss Anybody!
Honestly, Red Riding Hood Was Rotten!
No Kidding, Mermaids Are a Joke!
No Lie, I Acted Like a Beast!

Really, Rapunzel Needed a Haircut!
Seriously, Cinderella Is SO Annoying!
Seriously, Snow White Was SO Forgetful!
Truly, We Both Loved Beauty Dearly!
Trust Me, Jack's Beanstalk Stinks!

Super-cool stuff! Check out projects, games and lots more at www.capstonekids.com